VIA FOLIOS 102

A New Life with Bianca

Also by Frank Polizzi

All Around Town (2011)

A New Life with Bianca

Sonnets

Frank Polizzi

Illustrated with engravings by Michael McCurdy

Italian translations by Chiara Curtoni

Sicilian translations by Nino Provenzano

Afterword by Anthony Di Renzo

BORDIGHERA PRESS

Library of Congress Control Number: 2014944621

COVER ART
Michael McCurdy

Printed in the United States.

Published by
BORDIGHERA PRESS
John D. Calandra Italian American Institute
25 West 43rd Street, 17th Floor
New York, NY 10036

VIA FOLIOS 102
ISBN 978-1-59954-077-1

ACKNOWLEDGEMENTS

These poems, some in different versions or with different titles, have appeared in the following publications:

Feile-Festa , Spring 2007
All Around Town. Finishing Line Press (2011)

For my Sicilian grandparents who emigrated
to America at the turn of the 20th century:

Sebastiano and Antonina Polizzi
&
Paolo and Lucia Spata

Table of Contents

A New Life with Bianca

I

There was this pale woman in a dark café;
someone whispered her name to me – Bianca.
A white candle lit her face guiding my way,
and I sat opposite her replica.

In the pitted mirror among stolen rays,
it's like her silhouette began a reeler
for an indie movie in Astoria
just now blacked out by an aspiring waiter.

In my room the TV is an incessant spiel;
I open the next door to lather my face,
staring at the steam lines on the glass.

Later I finger the keyboard to send an e-mail,
scrolling her screen name and leave a trace,
then I'm back there sipping unsweet demitasse.

Figure 1

I

C'era poca luce nel bar, e una donna pallida;
Bianca il suo nome, sussurrò qualcuno.
Le illuminava il viso una candela candida
e mi accostai al suo riflesso, poco lontano.

Sullo specchio ammaccato tra i raggi rubati,
la sua silhouette pareva avviare
un film d'autore girato ad Astoria,
a tratti oscurato da un aspirante cameriere.

Nella mia stanza la tv è ciarliera;
vado di là ad insaponarmi la faccia,
fissando sul vetro le strisce di vapore.

Poi, per mandare un'e-mail sfioro la tastiera,
scorro il suo nome d'arte, lascio una traccia,
e rieccomi al Caffè, intento a sorseggiare.

I

Dintra un café ch'è scarsu illuminatu,
una cannila rischiara lu visu
di 'sta picciotta pallida. Iu di latu
'ntisi lu nomu Bianca. Un specchiu appisu

arroba luci e la so' facci puru.
Lu so' riflessu parsi accuminciari
un indi film giratu in Astoria.
Spraticu, un cammareri va bloccari.

'Nta la me' stanza la tv un si zitti.
'Nta l'atra trasu, la facci 'nsapunu,
vapuri d'acqua 'nta lu specchiu vitti.

Dopu m'assettu e un email priparu,
scopru lu nomu d'arti e lassu traccia.
Sugnu prisenti e pigghiu café amaru.

II

Felt like forever before seeing Bianca,
but it turned into our brief encounter.
So what was I to her, some sort of nebula
to be observed, then blown away in vapors.

Someone charmed her with his camera;
I wasn't wealthy, definitely not hipster.
Your face could have been drawn on majolica;
you were the stars to me in the exterior.

I sauntered along the East River bank
obsessing about the times we had embraced,
moments that mean more to me than the sunset.

Jumping over the rail was an option blank,
but lacking courage, some things can't be erased;
and I suffer twice, not to have, not to forget.

Figure 2

II

Sembrava un'eternità che non vedevo Bianca,
ma si mutò in un breve incontro.
Cos'ero mai per lei, una nebulosa da osservare,
presto dissolta in vapore.

Lui l'ammaliò con la macchina fotografica;
non ero ricco io, né tantomeno alla moda.
Il tuo viso un perfetto disegno su maiolica;
eri per me luce di stella nuda.

Lungo l'East River girovagavo
ossessionato dai nostri abbracci,
più preziosi per me del tramonto.

Il coraggio di saltar giù non l'avevo,
ma ci son cose che non scacci;
non avere, non dimenticare: doppio tormento.

II

Parsi n'eternità chi un vitti a Bianca.
N'incontru curtu fu, ma iu pi idda
chi cosa era? Nevula, pulviri di stidda
sciusciatu e poi squagghiatu 'nta lu nenti!

Cu 'ntentu e camera l'ammaliau
chiddu. Riccu e mudernu un'era iu.
Nta la maiolica la to' facci viu.
Luci di stidda eri tu pi mia.

Quasi currennu di E. River a latu
'mpazzutu pi quannu n'abbrazzamu,
mumenti chiù priziusi di un tramuntu.

Curaggiu unn'aiu pi moriri anniatu,
soffru dui voti. Nun pozzu scurdari
lu soccu vogghiu e mancu cancillari.

III

My passion for Bianca never ended
with her marriage to someone else, so hopeless.
Oh no, you weren't in the least disheartened;
I was in denial, full of pensiveness.

A medieval dreamer revisited,
you said in your role as modern sorceress.
I am standing on corners disquieted,
thinking about your exotic pearliness.

Killing time is easy when life is sucked out,
No juices to go on, *niente, nada,*
and I crawl out of my hole of a place.

I should take a trip, hear the locals sing out
"Girl from Ipanema," maybe dance a samba;
be content we're both part of the human race.

Figure 3

III

Mai finì la mia passione per Bianca, vitale
nonostante il suo matrimonio, così disperante.
Oh no, certo tu non stavi male;
io, fitto di pensieri, non volevo vedere niente.

Un nuovo tipo di sognatore medievale
mi definisti tu, moderna fattucchiera.
Inquieto in un angolo mi assale
il pensiero di te, perla bianca e rara.

Una vita prosciugata ammazza il tempo facilmente,
non c'è linfa per andare avanti, niente, nada,
e striscio fuori dal mio buco di tana.

Dovrei viaggiare, sentir cantar la gente
"La ragazza di Ipanema", ballare forse un samba;
accontentarmi di appartenere entrambi alla razza umana.

III

La passioni pi Bianca un mi finiu
cu lu so' matrimoniu. No spiranza,
mancu pi testa tu, a stu piniu.
Pinzusu nun criria a sta vilanza.

Un sonnu midievali mi dicisti
'nta lu to' rolu di maga muderna.
'Nta l'anguli mi fermu e penzu tristi
a st'esotica perla, e mi custerna.

Ammazzu tempu, mi manca la vita
nun haiu energia, ma nesciu di la tana.
Facissi un viaggiu, dunni un cantu invita.

A sentiri "La Picciotta di Ipanema",
mentri ballu la samba e su' cuntentu
chi semu tutti dui razza umana.

IV

It just took a couple of seconds, that's all,
and Bianca's husband was crushed in a car crash.
Like in *Run Lola Run*, where any thing can fall
different ways, one delayed step, all in a flash.

You were in mourning when I made the phone call;
saw you later dressed in black not for panache.
It was worse when you began to bawl,
I worry – you at the grave and weeping ash.

For some wild reason I ran home on remote,
sorry for your loss, but lucky he was gone;
still it would be a race to win, my milestone.

Divine a potion, search for an antidote,
but a chance moment is the *sine qua non*;
I waited a year and you were still alone.

Figure 4

IV

Bastarono un paio di secondi appena,
e il marito di Bianca morì in un incidente.
Come in *Corri Lola Corri*, la vita cambia scena
per un passo ritardato, imprevedibilmente.

Eri a lutto quando chiamai la mattina;
vestita di quel nero più cupo che elegante.
Ma peggio fu vedere la tua pena,
le tue lacrime alla tomba, salice piangente.

Senza ragione corsi fino a casa,
triste per te, e insieme fortunato;
ma la vera sfida non era vinta ancora.

Divinare pozioni e antidoti a iosa
non conta se il momento è sbagliato;
attesi un anno intero, e sola eri tuttora.

IV

Fu sulu dui sicunni e so' maritu
muriu scacciatu 'nta 'na cullisioni.
Curri Lola Curri un sbagliu, un lampu,
tuttu finiu 'nta 'na cunfisioni.

Eri di luttu quannu ti chiamavi,
senza superba, di niru vistuta
Ma peggiu quannu a lacrimi ti davi
Dulenti, 'nta la tomba a chiantu muta.

Si, dispiaciutu ma cuntentu puru.
Fici 'na cursa pazza pi la casa.
Vinciu sta sfida? La meta assicuru?

Divinu aiutu, cercu un talismanu,
ma l'opportunita' è l'esseziali.
E tu si sula e passa un'annu sanu.

V

There is a season for everything, so I've read;
Bianca and I were living together.
Our love was lush and fruity lying in bed
like the dessert wine we shared with each other.

The way you dance around the room in bright red;
life moves in you, your body round with water.
Cut to baby who joins us before we wed;
our film fades quicker than celluloid fire.

Years later, the next child arrives in marriage
and it seems as if we're more content again,
but all the rushes have changed to parenting.

Don't know if we should rewind to a new age
or just fast forward to something more urbane?
You and I were never big on focusing.

Figure 5

V

C'è un tempo per ogni cosa, recita il detto;
Bianca ed io vivevamo insieme.
Fruttato l'amore e lussureggiante a letto
come il vino dolce delle uve prime.

Danzavi nella stanza nel tuo rosso prediletto;
il tuo corpo tondo d'acqua della vita aveva il seme.
Fu prima delle nozze l'evento benedetto;
il nostro film incalza, veloce fiamma freme.

Anni dopo un altro figlio, e noi sposati
sembriamo di nuovo più contenti,
ma la scena è cambiata, siamo genitori.

Riavvolgere la pellicola a ciò che eravamo stati
o cercare nuove vie scorrendola in avanti?
Non siamo mai stati attenti spettatori.

V

C'è un tempu p'ogni cosa, haiu liggiutu,
e 'nta lu lettu ora Bianca ed iu
comu di un vinu in estasi vivutu,
cunsumamu cu lussu ogni disiu.

Di russu vivu tu balli vistuta,
si tunna, vita è in tia, nutricu aspetti.
Prima di maritari, e comu pagghia
stu nostru film pigghiau focu e squagghia.

N'atru nutricu dopu maritati,
pari chi semu ancora chiù cuntenti.
Canciaru li sceni, cu figghi 'mpignati.

Chi sacciu, 'ncuminciamu vita nova…
Passamu avanti in qualcosa chiù urbanu?
Pi fari piani un'amu datu prova.

VI

Italians mastered the art of flirtation,
so I thought of playing this ancient game.
What woman could endure infatuation
from a silly married man lacking any fame?

Someone, not too old or young, a sensation
who'd swoon when I said what a beautiful name.
Throw in blue moons, red flowers, good vibrations
of tunes from the American songbook, no shame.

My moment happened in the new MoMA
when an art instructor stood close by my side,
as we studied Gauguin's painting of *The Seed*...

I fancied she shared the same *faccia bella*;
we went to the *espresso* bar where I lied,
deleted her e-mail, when I had agreed.

Figure 6

VI

Gli italiani sono maestri nel corteggiare
ed io mi dilettai in questa antica trama.
Quale donna resiste all'ammiccare
di uno sciocco sposato e senza alcuna fama?

Non vecchia, né giovane, da inebriare
complimentando il nome suo bellissimo di dama.
Ci misi lune blu, fiori rossi, il vibrare
di canzoni americane, sfrontatezza estrema.

Il mio momento giunse al nuovo MoMa,
un'insegnante d'arte si mise accanto a me,
studiando il quadro di Gauguin *Il seme…*

Mi parve che lei avesse la stessa faccia bella;
ma al bar le mentii davanti a un caffè,
e cancellai la sua e-mail, quando non più insieme.

VI

L'Italiani maestri a lu curteggiu.
Penzu di usari chistu anticu iocu.
E quali donna un perdi lu punteggiu
cu unu maritatu, un veru cunta pocu?

No granni o nica, ma 'na senzazioni
chi sveni a un cumplimentu di bisognu.
Blu luni, ciuri russi, e lu vibrari
di toni americani, e nun mi vriognu.

Lu me' mumentu fu a nova MoMA,
cu 'na maestra d'arti a lu me' latu.
Puntau Gauguin, *The Seed*…, vota bona.

Suggirii ch'idda avia anchi facci bedda.
Emu a lu bar espresso e dda 'mbruggliai.
Cancillai l'email quannu accurdai.

VII

It was so real for Bianca, that I'm sure,
but she never dreamed I'd decipher her tryst.
It's hard to say why she did it, go figure;
should I sort out her pros and cons in a list?

A sudden rise in my temperature,
then cooling down in sweat as fine as the mist.
She said it was a silly trifle to obscure
things, made it seem less passionate she'd insist.

I debated alone – things remain the same,
didn't believe any more, except for her,
which was my mantra, standing under a cloud.

Without a choice, I prayed to Mnemosyne
to make me forget – need a change of weather,
but not a change of heart, no crying out loud.

Figure 7

VII

Per Bianca era un cosa vera, ne sono certo
ma non si sognava che avrei decifrato la sua tresca.
Difficile capirne i motivi, non sono esperto;
sui suoi pro e contro, meglio non mi accanisca.

Sentii caldo all'improvviso, il deserto
e poi il sudore, sottile bruma fresca.
Lei defini 'sciocchezza' quanto aveva inferto,
sminuendo una passione poco cavalleresca.

Mi dibattevo – che tutto restasse uguale infine,
non lo credevo più, ma lei in questa storia
rimaneva il mio mantra, sotto nuvole informi.

Non avevo scelta, pregai Mnemosine
di farmi dimenticare – dovevo cambiare aria,
ma non il cuore, e senza disperarmi.

VII

Bianca era certa di la sua avventura,
ma nun sunnava chi iu lu capia.
Difficili sapiri picchì, e allura
fazzu di si e no 'na lista mia.

Iu suru friddu, poi cavuru sentu.
Idda mi dissi chi nun ci fu nenti
pi oscurari cosi un c'è lu 'ntentu.
'Nsisti. "Nun fu passioni. Farsi mumenti".

Discurru sulu ma tuttu e` lu stissu
e chiu` nun criu, eccettu pi idda,
e divintau lu motto miu chissu.

Senza 'na scelta, preu a Nemosine,
quantu mi scordu. Aria haiu a canciari,
ma no lu cori, senza dispirari.

VIII

The children were older and we sought our youth;
they had apartments, lovers and dreams to live.
We were free walking naked (wasn't uncouth),
enjoyed sex openly and knew how to forgive.

Breast cancer increases, we read in some book,
with childbirth post thirty-five, risks positive.
Bianca's diagnosis turned into truth;
ironic our newborn love gauged negative.

The stages of her life induced her dying;
at the wake they said how beautiful she looked,
while I paced the bedroom floor, muttering why?

It's been a year now and I'm still not trying
to meet someone, friends plead, but CDs have me hooked,
as Nancy LaMott sings "Not a Day Goes By."

Figure 8

VIII

I figli erano grandi e cercammo la nostra giovinezza;
loro avevano case, amori e sogni da avverare.
Noi liberi camminavamo nudi (non era una stranezza),
ci godevamo il sesso e sapevamo perdonare.

Leggemmo che aumenta il rischio di tumore
dopo i trentacinque con la maternità.
Ironicamente, il neonato amore
rese il pericolo per Bianca una realtà.

Gli stadi della vita ne indussero la morte.
Alla veglia dicevano quanto era bella
io non sapevo darmi pace, né risposte ormai.

È passato un anno e me ne sto in disparte,
gli amici mi cercano, ma solo ascolto quella
canzone di Nancy LaMott, "Not a Day Goes By".

VIII

Circamu giuvintù! Li figghi granni
cu li so' sonni, amanti, apartamenti.
Nui circulamu in casa senza panni,
'mparamu a pirdunari. A sessu intenti.

La scienza dici, "Cancru 'Mpettu Avanza
Novi Matri Dopu Li Trentacincu'anni".
La tinta virita` a Bianca un scanza.
A chistu amuri ironicu, cunnanni!

Quannu fu morta, dintra lu tabbutu
paria bedda, dicianu tutti.
Passiu, stanza di lettu e quasi mutu

dicu picchi? Ed avi un annu! Un tornu
a 'ncuntrari qualcunu. CD attentu.
Nancy LaMott canta "Not a Day Goes By".

IX

We dreamed for reunion in *Paradiso*
before she died, planned like Dante and Beatrice.
Our love was like dancing an adagio,
but we managed to stay online, free access.

I google Bianca to make sure, you know,
she has name recognition on earth's surface.
The children and I rented a bungalow
and we reminisced, forgetting all the stress.

In Green-Wood, re-landmarked with her in the ground,
I prefer to see her under stars at night
yet still carry daily votives for my belle.

One eve, crashing this garden of death, no sound,
I'd thought to speed up life's process to unite,
but things would reverse, sending me back to hell.

Figure 9

IX

Sognammo di riunirci in Paradiso
prima che lei morisse, come Dante e Beatrice.
Il nostro amore era un passo a due indiviso,
ma ora siamo online, connessione veloce.

Cerco su Google se di Bianca ravviso
il nome in terra. Coi figli inseguo pace
insieme a loro mi sono arreso
ai ricordi, terapia guaritrice.

A Green-Wood, nobilitato dalle sue spoglie,
preferisco andarci nella notte stellata,
e ancora alla mia bella porto candele.

Una sera, in questo muto giardino senza foglie,
pensai di raggiungerla e farla finita,
ma non lei, l'inferno mi avrebbe accolto crudele.

IX

Sunnamu riuniri 'mParadisu
prima chi morsi, comu Danti e Biatrici.
St'amuri, fu un ballu lentu, spisu.
Stettimu online senza sacrifici.

Iu google Bianca, vogghiu chi lu nomu
è canusciutu 'nterra. Ora affittamu
'ncampagna cu li figghi 'na casuzza.
Parramu di ricordi. Forsi sanamu.

Di terra a Green-Wood avi 'na fedda.
Prifirisciu vidilla sutta li stiddi,
e portu ancora vuti a la me' bedda.

Na sira circai morti dispiratu.
Silenziu. Cridia chiù prima vidilla.
Fui a lu 'nfernu chiù 'nfunnu ammuttatu.

AFTERWORD

A New Life with Bianca

"TO TRY TO WRITE LOVE," Roland Barthes observes in *A Lover's Discourse* (1977), a collection of fragments on desire, delay and despair, "is to confront the muck of language; that region of hysteria where language is both too much and too little, excessive (by the limitless expansion of the ego, by emotive submersion) and impoverished (by the codes on which love diminishes and levels it)."

Waiting in a Parisian café for an elusive lover, Barthes kills time and wrestles with anxiety and jealousy by reading Goethe's *The Sorrows of Young Werther* and meditating on the history of European Romanticism. This philosophical exercise fails to console him. Barthes realizes that he is not only an animal driven by irrational biology but also a hostage to and a dupe of an intellectually bankrupt but emotionally manipulative literary tradition. Nevertheless, Barthes assembles the pieces of a shattered life into a temporarily meaningful pattern. In the process, he discovers beauty in—and creates a work of art suitable for—an irreparably broken culture.

Frank Polizzi, a Sicilian American poet, does the same in *A New Life with Bianca*. This sequence of nine interconnected sonnets is simultaneously a coroner's inquest on love and loss and an archeological dig of the Italian sonnet tradition. Written in English and then translated into Italian and Sicilian by respectively Chiara Curtoni and Nino Provenzano, the collection is also a haunting palimpsest on the beauty and limitations of language. Michael McCurdy's haunting engravings enhance this book's elegant melancholy.

Modeled after Dante's *La Vita Nuova*, Petrarch's *Canzoniere*, and Spenser's *Amoretti*, *A New Life with Bianca* chronicles a young man's passion for a widow his age, from their first encounter in a café and initial courtship, to their shotgun wedding and comfortable domesticity, to her untimely death from breast cancer. At every stage of their relationship, the speaker—an Italian American, latter-day bohemian who reads poetry, watches indie films and frequents the MoMA—tries to express and interpret his feelings through the medium of culture. The gap between art and experience, however, proves too wide.

Polizzi explores this ontological chasm with a rock climber's care and precision. As his eye detects every foothold and fault line, his mind processes ancient geological patterns. By turns comic and tragic (often both at once), the provocative interplay between immediate concrete sensation and delayed abstract contemplation distinguishes Polizzi's work. Rather than stay within the familiar hermeneutical circle of his ethnic neighborhood or take a Fulbright tour of *Bell' Italia*, his poetry confronts the baffling complexities of postmodernity.

A New Life with Bianca captures the pain and paradox of romantic love in our artificial and excruciatingly self-conscious society, a culture of canned laughter, anonymous chatrooms, knee-jerk cynicism and media saturation. Shakespeare's Orlando expresses his obsession for Rosalind by nailing sonnets to every tree in Arden Forest. Polizzi's sonneteer deals with his passion for Bianca by checking e-mail and listening to "The Girl from Ipanema" on an iPod. At the same time, he quixotically strives to emulate the courtly tradition of Italian love poetry. As he confides during the early stages of their affair:

> Italians mastered the art of flirtation
> so I thought of playing the ancient game.
> What woman could endure infatuation
> from a silly married man lacking any fame?

Polizzi humorously contrasts Astoria, Queens with Florence, Italy, but his purpose is serious. By juxtaposing twenty-first century America and thirteenth-century Italy, he redefines both epochs and recovers the Italian sonnet's shocking and experimental technique. His guide, however, is not the Tuscan Dante Alighieri but his fellow Sicilian, Iacopo da Lentinti, whose poetry is echoed and paraphrased in *A New Life with Bianca*. Polizzi's choice of mentor is apt.

The sonnet was born in early thirteenth-century Sicily, at the court of the cultivated and cosmopolitan Frederick II. Located at the crossroads of Mediterranean civilization, Sicily had absorbed the scientific advances of Islamic North Africa, along with the chivalric habits typically found in the troubadour poetry of southern France. Both currents converged to create the Sicilian sonnet, which fused courtly sophistication and an almost judicial taste for argument and precise form. Such dialectical poetry suited Frederick, whose passion for classical rhetoric, Greek philosophy and Roman law complemented a commitment to empiricism, experimentation and exploration.

Trained as lawyers and civil servants, Sicilian poets deposed and cross-examined the Provençal troubadour tradition that they had inherited from the Normans. They questioned the assumptions behind courtly love and sought to discipline their passions through inquiry and debate. Masters of deliberative procedure, they also valued rules of order. They invented a new poetic form, therefore, governed by the strictest formal properties. Consisting of fourteen lines, it was divided into an octave (eight opening lines) and a sestet (six closing lines); the division between the two sections being marked with a *volta*, or turn of thought. Its regular rhyme scheme demanded and enforced concentration. The Sicilians called their invention a *sonnetto* ("little song") but it was not lyrical. Asymmetrical and self-divided, it was suited to meditative logic rather than music.

As Stephen Burt and David Mikics note in their introduction to *The Art of the Sonnet* (Harvard University Press, 2010), the sonnet "summarizes, begs, proves, and experiments; it calculates its effects, and turns in on itself with patient intent." Its first great practitioner was Iacopo da Lentini (ca. 1210 – ca. 1260), whom Dante in the *Purgatorio* apostrophizes as 'l Notaro. A notary in Frederick's court, he was a colleague of the emperor's secretary Pietro della Vigna, who appears in the *Inferno*'s Forest of Suicides. Like John Donne, Lentini weds hothouse eroticism and metaphysical paradox. Even when his thoughts are riddling, however, his sonnets blaze with the lucid fire and sun-drenched colors of Sicily. Each word is as polished as the majolica tiles in Caltagirone's fabled staircase.

The Sicilian sonnet was a turning point in Western poetry: the lyric purified itself and became a reflection on reflection. According to Burt and Mikics, it also marked a profound shift in Western consciousness: "The sonnet form thrives on, and fosters, debate within the self, a thorny internal monologue. But it also reins in, and rounds off, thinking, and so makes inwardness complete and absolute." Our attempts to overcome isolation through poetry, therefore, are doomed to reinforce it.

This dilemma sounds remarkably contemporary. Modernity's political and scientific revolutions, critics claim, forever severed sign and signifier. We are all condemned to pine for meaning in Viktor Shklovsky's prison-house of language. Postmodernism merely added security cameras and Muzak to this semiotic gulag.

Frank Polizzi's allusive poetry challenges this view. His dialogue with past Italian sonneteers shows the continuity in discontinuity. When he mourns for Bianca, he also mourns for Beatrice, Laura, and Stella. The poet's lament is old as that of Orpheus for Eurydice. We have never sung to resolve our feelings but to express them. Catharsis and enlightenment are irrelevant.

Even so, *A New Life with Bianca* shows how poetry has become fugitive and transient in a world of rapid-fire texts and 140-character Tweets. Unlike Shakespeare, Polizzi's sonneteer cannot tell his beloved:

> Not marble nor the gilded monuments
> Of princes shall outlive this powerful rhyme,
> But you shall shine more bright in these contents
> Than unswept stone besmeared with sluttish time.

The best he can do is "google Bianca to make sure, you know, / she has name recognition on earth's surface." When a culture refuses to provide even the flimsiest shelter against death and oblivion, poetry assumes the shelf life of milk. But is a love note any less precious, Polizzi asks, because it is written in sand and doomed to be erased by the tide? Impermanence is the source of all beauty.

ANTHONY DI RENZO
Ithaca College

FRANK POLIZZI is the editor of *Feile-Festa*, a multicultural, literary arts journal (http://www.medcelt.org/feile-festa/). He has worked as a Vista Volunteer in New London, CT, an English teacher on the original staff to reopen Townsend Harris HS at Queens College and the Head of Reference and Instructional Services at the Hormann Library of Wagner College. His poems and stories have appeared in *The Archer*, *Bitterroot*, *Electric Acorn* (Dublin Writers), *Mudfish*, *Paterson Literary Review*, *Wired Art* and others. The Guild of Italian American Actors (GIAA) accepted his one-act play, *By the Light of a Barber Pole* for its reading series in 2009. Two years later, Finishing Line Press published *All Around Town*, his poems exploring Sicilian American roots and experiences in NYC. Several chapter/stories were published from his novel, *A Pity Beyond All Telling*, and one of them was shortlisted for the Fish Prize in Ireland. Frank is currently seeking a publisher for a new novel, *Somewhere in the Stars*, which made the 2014 Long list of the UK publisher, Lightship, for its "First Novel Prize."

CONTRIBUTORS

DR. CHIARA CURTONI is a native of Turin, Italy, graduating magna cum laude from the Faculty of Literature and Philosophy at the University of Turin. She taught at the University of Liberal Arts / DAMS (University of Turin) and for the PhD program in Technology and Multimedia Communication. She lives in New York, where she is the Language Program Coordinator at the Italian American Committee on Education. Also a musician, she performed extensively as a jazz-pop singer in Europe and USA.

NINO PROVENZANO has had two poetry collections published by Legas Press: *Vinissi... / I'd Love to Come...* and *Turno / The Return.* He is currently the Vice President of *Arba Sicula*, an organization promoting Sicilian culture worldwide. *The New York Times* published two articles on his work promoting Sicilian poetry in America. He provided Sicilian translations for the film, *MAC*, directed by John Torturro, and he worked with director, Spike Lee, in preparing John Leguizamo for his role in the film, *Son of Sam.*

MICHAEL MCCURDY has illustrated and authored books, such as *Toward the Light; The Old Man and the Fiddle*, and *Trapped by the Ice*: *Shackleton's Amazing Antarctic Adventure.* He has illustrated books for other authors, including *The Winged Life: The Poetry of Henry David Thoreau*, David Mamet's *American Buffalo* and the *John Muir Library Series*. Michael's engravings and book design for Howard Norman's *The Owl-Scatterer* was chosen by *The New York Times* as one of the Ten Best Illustrated Children's Books of 1986, and again in 1996 for Ann Whitford Paul's *The Seasons Sewn: The Year in Patchwork.*

ANTHONY DI RENZO teaches writing at Ithaca College. His books, such as *Bitter Greens: Essays on Food, Politics, and History from the Imperial Kitchen* (State University of New York Press, 2010) and *Trinàcria: A Tale of Bourbon Sicily* (Guernica Editions, 2013), satirize the ongoing culture war between Italian humanism and American business and technology. As Pasquino, Rome's talking statue, he contributes a monthly column to San Francisco's *L'Italo-Americano*.

VIA FOLIOS

A refereed book series dedicated to the culture of Italians and Italian Americans.

FRANK POLIZZI. *A New Life with Bianca.* Vol 102 Poetry. $12
GIL FAGIANI. *Stone Walls.* Vol 101 Poetry. $14
LOUISE DESALVO. *Casting Off.* Vol 100 Fiction. $22
MARY JO BONA. *I stop waiting for You.* Vol 99 Poetry. $12
RACHEL GUIDO DEVRIES. *Stati zitt, Josie.* Vol 98 Children's Literature. $8
GRACE CAVALIERI. *The Mandate of Heaven.* Vol 97 Poetry. $14
MARISA FRASCA. *Via incanto.* Vol 96 Poetry. $12
DOUGLAS GLADSTONE. *Carving a Niche for Himself.* Vol 95 History. $12
MARIA TERRONE. *Eye to Eye.* Vol 94 Poetry. $14
CONSTANCE SANCETTA. *Here in Cerchio* Vol 93 Local History. $15
MARIA MAZZIOTTI GILLAN. *Ancestors' Song* Vol 92 Poetry. $14
DARRELL FUSARO. *What if Godzilla Just Wanted a Hug?* Vol ? Essays. $TBA
MICHAEL PARENTI. *Waiting for Yesterday: Pages from a Street Kid's Life.* Vol 90 Memoir. $15
ANNIE LANZILOTTO, *Schistsong*, Vol. 89. Poetry, $15
EMANUEL DI PASQUALE, *Love Lines*, Vol. 88. Poetry, $10
CAROSONE & LOGIUDICE. *Our Naked Lives* Vol 87 Essays. $15
JAMES PERICONI. *Strangers in a Strange Land: A Survey of Italian-Language American Books.*
    Vol. 86. Book History. $24
DANIELA GIOSEFFI, *Escaping La Vita Della Cucina*, Vol. 85. Essays & Creative Writing. $22
MARIA FAMÀ, *Mystics in the Family*, Vol. 84. Poetry, $10
ROSSANA DEL ZIO, *From Bread and Tomatoes to Zuppa di Pesce "Ciambotto"*, Vol. 83. $15
LORENZO DELBOCA, *Polentoni*, Vol. 82. Italian Studies, $15
SAMUEL GHELLI, *A Reference Grammar*, Vol. 81. Italian Language. $36
ROSS TALARICO, *Sled Run*, Vol. 80. Fiction. $15
FRED MISURELLA, *Only Sons*, Vol. 79. Fiction. $14
FRANK LENTRICCHIA, *The Portable Lentricchia*, Vol. 78. Fiction. $16
RICHARD VETERE, *The Other Colors in a Snow Storm*, Vol. 77. Poetry. $10
GARIBALDI LAPOLLA, *Fire in the Flesh*, Vol. 76 Fiction & Criticism. $25
GEORGE GUIDA, *The Pope Stories*, Vol. 75 Prose. $15
ROBERT VISCUSI, *Ellis Island*, Vol. 74. Poetry. $28
ELENA GIANINI BELOTTI, *The Bitter Taste of Strangers Bread*, Vol. 73, Fiction, $24
PINO APRILE, *Terroni*, Vol. 72, Italian Studies, $20
EMANUEL DI PASQUALE, *Harvest*, Vol. 71, Poetry, $10
ROBERT ZWEIG, *Return to Naples*, Vol. 70, Memoir, $16
AIROS & CAPPELLI, *Guido*, Vol. 69, Italian/American Studies, $12
FRED GARDAPHÉ, *Moustache Pete is Dead! Long Live Moustache Pete!*, Vol. 67, Literature/Oral
    History, $12
PAOLO RUFFILLI, *Dark Room/Camera oscura*, Vol. 66, Poetry, $11
HELEN BAROLINI, *Crossing the Alps*, Vol. 65, Fiction, $14
COSMO FERRARA, *Profiles of Italian Americans*, Vol. 64, Italian Americana, $16
GIL FAGIANI, *Chianti in Connecticut*, Vol. 63, Poetry, $10
BASSETTI & D'ACQUINO, *Italic Lessons*, Vol. 62, Italian/American Studies, $10

Bordighera Press is an imprint of Bordighera, Incorporated, an independently owned not-for-profit
scholarly organization that has no legal affiliation with the University of Central Florida or with
The John D. Calandra Italian American Institute, Queens College/CUNY.

CAVALIERI & PASCARELLI, Eds., *The Poet's Cookbook*, Vol. 61, Poetry/Recipes, $12

EMANUEL DI PASQUALE, *Siciliana*, Vol. 60, Poetry, $8

NATALIA COSTA, Ed., *Bufalini*, Vol. 59, Poetry. $18.

RICHARD VETERE, *Baroque*, Vol. 58, Fiction. $18.

LEWIS TURCO, *La Famiglia/The Family*, Vol. 57, Memoir, $15

NICK JAMES MILETI, *The Unscrupulous*, Vol. 56, Humanities, $20

BASSETTI, ACCOLLA, D'AQUINO, *Italici: An Encounter with Piero Bassetti*, Vol. 55, Italian Studies, $8

GIOSE RIMANELLI, *The Three-legged One*, Vol. 54, Fiction, $15

CHARLES KLOPP, *Bele Antiche Stòrie*, Vol. 53, Criticism, $25

JOSEPH RICAPITO, *Second Wave*, Vol. 52, Poetry, $12

GARY MORMINO, *Italians in Florida*, Vol. 51, History, $15

GIANFRANCO ANGELUCCI, *Federico F.*, Vol. 50, Fiction, $15

ANTHONY VALERIO, *The Little Sailor*, Vol. 49, Memoir, $9

ROSS TALARICO, *The Reptilian Interludes*, Vol. 48, Poetry, $15

RACHEL GUIDO DE VRIES, *Teeny Tiny Tino's Fishing Story*, Vol. 47, Children's Literature, $6

EMANUEL DI PASQUALE, *Writing Anew*, Vol. 46, Poetry, $15

MARIA FAMÀ, *Looking For Cover*, Vol. 45, Poetry, $12

ANTHONY VALERIO, *Toni Cade Bambara's One Sicilian Night*, Vol. 44, Poetry, $10

EMANUEL CARNEVALI, Dennis Barone, Ed., *Furnished Rooms*, Vol. 43, Poetry, $14

BRENT ADKINS, et al., Ed., *Shifting Borders, Negotiating Places*, Vol. 42, Proceedings, $18

GEORGE GUIDA, *Low Italian*, Vol. 41, Poetry, $11

GARDAPHÈ, GIORDANO, TAMBURRI, *Introducing Italian Americana*, Vol. 40, Italian/American Studies, $10

DANIELA GIOSEFFI, *Blood Autumn/Autunno di sangue*, Vol. 39, Poetry, $15/$25

FRED MISURELLA, *Lies to Live by*, Vol. 38, Stories, $15

STEVEN BELLUSCIO, *Constructing a Bibliography*, Vol. 37, Italian Americana, $15

ANTHONY JULIAN TAMBURRI, Ed., *Italian Cultural Studies 2002*, Vol. 36, Essays, $18

BEA TUSIANI, *con amore*, Vol. 35, Memoir, $19

FLAVIA BRIZIO-SKOV, Ed., *Reconstructing Societies in the Aftermath of War*, Vol. 34, History, $30

TAMBURRI, et al., Eds., *Italian Cultural Studies 2001*, Vol. 33, Essays, $18

ELIZABETH G. MESSINA, Ed., *In Our Own Voices*, Vol. 32, Italian/American Studies, $25

STANISLAO G. PUGLIESE, *Desperate Inscriptions*, Vol. 31, History, $12

HOSTERT & TAMBURRI, Eds., *Screening Ethnicity*, Vol. 30, Italian/American Culture, $25

G. PARATI & B. LAWTON, Eds., *Italian Cultural Studies*, Vol. 29, Essays, $18

HELEN BAROLINI, *More Italian Hours*, Vol. 28, Fiction, $16

FRANCO NASI, Ed., *Intorno alla Via Emilia*, Vol. 27, Culture, $16

ARTHUR L. CLEMENTS, *The Book of Madness & Love*, Vol. 26, Poetry, $10

JOHN CASEY, et al., *Imagining Humanity*, Vol. 25, Interdisciplinary Studies, $18

ROBERT LIMA, *Sardinia/Sardegna*, Vol. 24, Poetry, $10

DANIELA GIOSEFFI, *Going On*, Vol. 23, Poetry, $10

ROSS TALARICO, *The Journey Home*, Vol. 22, Poetry, $12

EMANUEL DI PASQUALE, *The Silver Lake Love Poems*, Vol. 21, Poetry, $7

JOSEPH TUSIANI, *Ethnicity*, Vol. 20, Poetry, $12

JENNIFER LAGIER, *Second Class Citizen*, Vol. 19, Poetry, $8

FELIX STEFANILE, *The Country of Absence*, Vol. 18, Poetry, $9

PHILIP CANNISTRARO, *Blackshirts*, Vol. 17, History, $12

LUIGI RUSTICHELLI, Ed., *Seminario sul racconto*, Vol. 16, Narrative, $10

LEWIS TURCO, *Shaking the Family Tree*, Vol. 15, Memoirs, $9

LUIGI RUSTICHELLI, Ed., *Seminario sulla drammaturgia*, Vol. 14, Theater/Essays, $10

FRED GARDAPHÈ, *Moustache Pete is Dead! Long Live Moustache Pete!*, Vol. 13, Oral Literature, $10

JONE GAILLARD CORSI, *Il libretto d'autore*, 1860–1930, Vol. 12, Criticism, $17

HELEN BAROLINI, *Chiaroscuro: Essays of Identity*, Vol. 11, Essays, $15

PICARAZZI & FEINSTEIN, Eds., *An African Harlequin in Milan*, Vol. 10, Theater/Essays, $15

JOSEPH RICAPITO, *Florentine Streets & Other Poems*, Vol. 9, Poetry, $9

FRED MISURELLA, *Short Time*, Vol. 8, Novella, $7

NED CONDINI, *Quartettsatz*, Vol. 7, Poetry, $7

ANTHONY JULIAN TAMBURRI, Ed., *Fuori: Essays by Italian/American Lesbians and Gays*, Vol. 6, Essays, $10

ANTONIO GRAMSCI, P. Verdicchio, Trans. & Intro. , *The Southern Question*, Vol. 5, Social Criticism, $5

DANIELA GIOSEFFI, *Word Wounds & Water Flowers*, Vol. 4, Poetry, $8

WILEY FEINSTEIN, *Humility's Deceit: Calvino Reading Ariosto Reading Calvino*, Vol. 3, Criticism, $10

PAOLO A. GIORDANO, Ed., *Joseph Tusiani: Poet, Translator, Humanist*, Vol. 2, Criticism, $25

ROBERT VISCUSI, *Oration Upon the Most Recent Death of Christopher Columbus*, Vol. 1, Poetry, $3

.

www.ingramcontent.com/pod-product-compliance
Lightning Source LLC
Chambersburg PA
CBHW032057040426
42449CB00007B/1116